MUMMIES

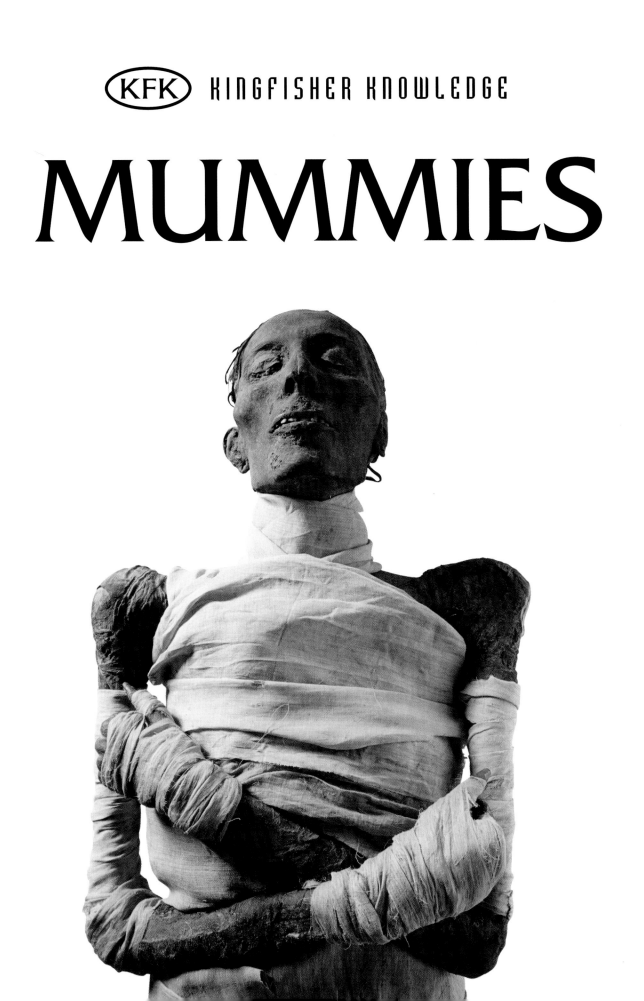

KFK KINGFISHER KNOWLEDGE

MUMMIES

John Malam

Foreword by
Ron Beckett and Gerald Conlogue

KINGFISHER
BOSTON

Senior editor: Carron Brown
Coordinating editor: Caitlin Doyle
Designers: Mark Bristow, Peter Clayman, Carol Ann Davis
Picture research manager: Cee Weston-Baker
DTP coordinator: Sarah Pfitzner
DTP operator: Primrose Burton
Senior production controller: Deborah Otter
Proofreader: Sheila Clewley
Artwork archivists: Wendy Allison, Jenny Lord

KINGFISHER
a Houghton Mifflin Company imprint
222 Berkeley Street
Boston, Massachusetts 02116
www.houghtonmifflinbooks.com

First published by Kingfisher in 2003
10 9 8 7 6 5 4 3 2 1

1TR/0603/TWP/MA(MA)/130ENSOMA

LIBRARY OF CONGRESS CATALOGING-IN-PUBLICATION DATA
Malam, John, 1957–
    Mummies / John Malam.—1st ed.
      p. cm.—(Kingfisher knowledge)
    Includes index.
    Contents: Two ways to make a mummy—Egypt, the land of
  mummies—Mummy world—Mummies today.
    1. Mummies—Juvenile literature. [1. Mummies.] I. Title. II. Series.

GT3340.M35 2003
393'.3—dc21   2003044630
ISBN 0-7534-5623-0

Printed in Singapore

NOTE TO READERS

The web site addresses listed in this book are correct at the time of publishing. However, due to the ever-changing nature of the Internet, web site addresses and content can change. Web sites can contain links that are unsuitable for children. The publisher cannot be held responsible for changes in web site addresses or content or for information obtained through third-party web sites. We strongly advise that Internet searches should be supervised by an adult.

INFORMATION PANEL KEY:

web sites and further reading

career paths

places to visit

Contents

Foreword

Why are we so fascinated by mummies? At first glance it is the "stuff" of mummies—the artifacts, the gold, the elaborately decorated coffins. It all seems so mystical. As we look closer we begin to see the person that is the mummy itself. We are drawn to its physical appearance and then to the face. We wonder what where they like? Did they have a family? What did they do in their life? How did they die? What was important to them? There are so many questions to be answered. As we look even more closely we begin to realize that these mummies were eyewitnesses to history and to the ancient times in which they lived. Looking at a mummy and all that surrounds it is like going back in time, taking an impossible journey back to days past.

We can learn so much about these ancient times from mummies. Too often history is written by conquerors. What we often get is a picture of an ancient culture as seen through the eyes and prejudices of people who were at war with them. Through the careful study of mummies—the eyewitnesses to their times—we can better understand what was important to these ancient people. We find that they were a lot like us. We can learn about their lives, the diseases that afflicted them, whether or not they were peaceful or warlike, hunters or farmers. We can learn about their art, their technology, and the tools they used. We can find clues about their style of government and social structure. We often learn that they cared about their loved ones and respected the dead just like we do today. We learn that peoples of times past were not living a bleak or bland life, but instead a life full of culture, color, belief systems, and music—much like we live today.

In this book, *Mummies,* you will travel around the globe and through time, seeing how ancient, and not so ancient, cultures cared for their dead. You will learn why people were mummified and will be amazed at the similarities and the differences. Some were mummified to preserve the body for use in an afterlife, while others were mummified to keep a loved one "nearby." Imagine the care with which parents prepared their children after their death, longing to somehow hold onto them. Still others were mummified to represent and perpetuate an idea. As you read this book try to imagine yourself in a time machine traveling back to visit members of the human race and to learn about how they lived and what they cared about. While the environments in which humans live have changed, expressions of life—and death— remain much the same. As you compare and contrast what was important to them—all those years ago—you may find that, fundamentally, we are more alike than different.

Ron Beckett & Gerald Conlogue
Co-Directors, Bioanthropology Research Institute at Quinnipiac University, Hamden, Connecticut

CHAPTER 1

Two ways to make a mummy

In ancient Egypt teams of embalmers made mummies. First they washed a dead body and then they cut a slit in one side of the body so that most of the innards could be pulled out. A hook was pushed inside a nostril and into the skull and then twisted to break the brain into pieces to be drained through the nose. The body was then covered with salts and left to dry—after which the body cavity was packed to restore its shape. Finally, the body was wrapped from head to toe in linen strips.

Nature does it differently—a body can be cast into a cold, wet peat bog, buried in a hot, dry desert, left at the top of a mountain, or entombed in an icy glacier. In all of these places nature can make mummies out of people and animals.

What is a mummy?

To put it simply, a mummy is the dead body of a person or an animal that has been preserved. Death may have robbed the body of life—the power to see, hear, touch, speak, and taste—but it does not mean an end to the body itself. Its mortal remains have not been consumed by worms or reduced to ash in a funeral pyre. Instead it has been saved from decay and has survived to the present day.

▲ Inside this carefully wrapped and decorated bundle is the body of a cat mummified in ancient Egypt. Perhaps it was a family pet buried with its owner so that it could join him or her in the afterlife.

The true meaning of the word "mummy"

The word "mummy" was first used to describe preserved bodies in ancient Egypt. However, "mummy" has come to be used for any preserved body, no matter where it comes from, how it was made, or how old it is. The origin of the word "mummy" is something of a mystery. For years it has been linked with the Arabic word *mummiya* (or *mummia*), which means "bitumen" (a sticky, black, tarlike substance). It was once thought that Egyptian mummies had turned black because the embalmers coated them with *mummiya*, from which it was thought that Europeans invented the word "mummy."

However, recent work by chemists suggests an alternative origin. When they analyzed the blackened resins on the bodies of Egyptian mummies, they found it was made from a mixture of ingredients that usually included tree resins, plant oils, animal fats, and a lot of beeswax. The Eygyptian word for "wax" was *mum*—it could be that this is the true origin of the word "mummy."

◀ This deliberately mummified body of the ancient Egyptian pharoah Tuthmosis IV wrapped in linen strips is how most people imagine a mummy to look.

Mummies made by human hands

Some mummies, such as most from ancient Egypt, were made intentionally. They are artificial mummies—bodies preserved deliberately in an attempt to stop the from rotting. The Egyptians were not the only people t practice mummy making—or, to give it another name "embalming" (when a dead body is treated with oils and spices to prevent its decay). People from as far apart as Chile and China also mummified bodies. The question is: "Why?" For some, such as the Egyptians, mummification was thought to be essential if a person was to live again after they had died. Because they believed in resurrection—that a person's body comes back to life after death—the body itself had to be saved. In other cultures bodies were preserved so that people could keep their ancestors with them, talking to them as if they were still alive.

▼ This is the body of a young girl who died in Peru around 500 years ago. Her finders called her Juanita. She was buried high up in the mountains, where the dry, freezing conditions preserved her. She is a natural mummy.

Mummies made by nature

Under certain conditions the forces of nature preserve the corpses of people and animals, turning them into natural mummies. These account for the worlds oldest—as well as the youngest—mummies. While the body of a mammoth might date back tens of thousands of years the remains of a mountaineer or an Arctic explorer may only be around one century old. Despite the age difference, these mummies have something in common— ice. Locked inside glaciers or frozen ground, the process of decay stops, and organic material is preserved in incredible detail.

It is not only cold temperatures that can make mummies. The world's hot, dry deserts suck the fluids out of bodies, reducing them to skin and bones. Even watery places, such as peat bogs, can transform a body into a mummy.

Mummies are time travelers

How should we think about mummies? Should we feel nervous because we are looking at dead bodies? Is it right for people to remove them from their resting places, probe them with scientific instruments, and put them on display in museums? These are important questions, and they are not easy to answer (see page 43). People today like to think that they are living in an educated time. There is no doubt that the people whose preserved bodies we find so fascinating thought exactly the same way about the world in which they lived. They could not possibly know that future generations would find them as interesting as we do now. We should think of mummies as time travelers—bodies that have lost the power of speech but that can still tell us about themselves and their lost worlds.

▶ Archaeologists carefully remove the mummies of a group of Chachapoyas (Cloud People) from their mountain burial place. The Chachapoyas of Peru lived alongside the Incas in the 1400s. Their bodies were wrapped in cloth and buried in mountain caves, where they slowly dried out and became mummies.

The world's first mummy makers

Thousands of years ago the northern coast of Chile was inhabited by fishing people. We call them the Chinchorro people—after Chinchorro beach where remains of their culture have been found. "Chinchorro" is an old Spanish word meaning "fishing nets." We have no way of knowing what these ancient people called themselves because they lived in a prehistoric time, a time before writing. However, they have left us something else—the world's oldest artificial mummies. The Chinchorro people were the first mummy makers.

Discovery of the Chinchorro mummies

As long ago as 1917 archaeologists knew that ancient mummies could be found in Chile. What they did not know was how old the odd-looking bodies uncovered at Chinchorro were. This changed in 1983 when workmen disturbed a long-forgotten cemetery, from which 96 mummies were excavated. To everyone's surprise the oldest turned out to have been made 7,000 years ago, around 5000 B.C. The Chinchorro preserved their dead in this way until the 1700s B.C., and then they began to make mummy bundles (see pages 38–39).

◄ This Chinchorro mummy's clay mask shows how the mummy makers of ancient Chile gave faces to the dead. Perhaps they believed that in a life after death the clay features would come to life, allowing the person to function normally once again.

► This group of clay-covered Chinchorro mummies is displayed in a museum to look how they did when they were found in the ground. Because they were buried with goods they would have used when they were alive, such as food and items used for fishing (harpoons and hooks made of bone), this is evidence that they believed in an afterlife—though what form it took is not known.

Mummy making the Chinchorro way

The Chinchorro had a unique way of making mummies. They slit open a body's abdomen, took out its insides, and then stripped the skin and flesh off of the bones (the skin was kept but the flesh was not). The brain was also removed. Then—and this is the incredible part—the body shape was put back together. Sticks were used to reinforce its spine, arms, and legs, and a thick layer of clay and plant fibers was molded onto the bones to form the shape of the body. Once the body had been remade the person's real skin was stretched over it. Sea lion skin was used to fill the gaps.

Paint, masks, and wigs to make the body beautiful

After the skin had been put on the body it was covered with a thin layer of ash paste that dried into a smooth, hard surface. It was then ready to be transformed into an image of beauty, as if it was a living being once again. The first Chinchorro mummies were painted black, and the later ones were painted red. Many were given clay masks with delicately modeled faces, and some wore clay helmets or long wigs of human hair.

▲ The fact that the Chinchorro mummies were repainted is evidence that they were not buried right away. It seems they were displayed out in the open for a while and were given new coats of paint as old ones wore off. Eventually they were placed in graves in cemeteries.

Ötzi—the man in ice

When a man's body was found in the ice of a mountain glacier in northern Italy in 1991, he was at first thought to be the victim of a recent accident. Then rescuers saw that his clothes were made of leather and grass and that he carried a bow, arrows, and a copper ax. It was clear that he had died a long time ago, and somehow his body and possessions had been preserved.

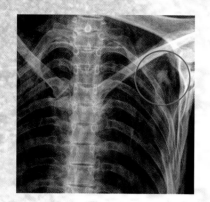

▲ In 2001 scientists in Italy X-rayed Ötzi's body. They found an 84-in.-long flint arrowhead (circled) lodged behind his left shoulder blade. It was a clue to how he had died, although why he had been shot, and by whom, is a mystery.

A name for the body

He is known by several names—the Iceman (because he was found in ice), Similaun Man (after the mountain pass where he was discovered), and Ötzi (a nickname invented by an Austrian reporter who mixed "Ötztal"— the region where the body was found—with "yeti"— a legendary mountain creature). We will never know Ötzi's real name, but scientists have learned a lot about him and the prehistoric world in which he lived and died by examining his body and possessions.

A prehistoric time capsule

Ötzi is one of the world's greatest archaeological discoveries. He is one of the oldest complete humans ever found and one of the world's oldest natural mummies. Radiocarbon tests on his body reveal that he is around 5,300 years old. This means that he lived in a period known as the Copper Age—the time when people in Europe used metal for the first time to make tools and weapons.

Among the 70 objects found with Ötzi was a flat-bladed ax made of copper, which was a very advanced tool for the time. There was also a bow with a quiver of 14 arrows, a leather pouch with flints and tinder for fire lighting, a flint dagger, and a wooden-framed backpack. He wore leather leggings, a goatskin coat, a bearskin hat, a grass cape, and leather shoes stuffed with grass to keep his feet warm. His skin was decorated with more than 50 tattoos. Ötzi and his remarkable objects show what prehistoric people in Europe wore and what they carried with them.

▶ After being shot the Iceman managed to pull the arrow shaft from his shoulder, but the flint arrowhead stayed in the wound. It was a serious injury. Bleeding, he walked high up into the icy mountains, where he died.

How did Ötzi die?

Aged around 46 and suffering from arthritis in his joints, Ötzi would have been thought of as an old man at the time, but this did not stop one or more people from attacking him. His right hand was badly cut, possibly in a fight, and he was shot in the back. He fled to the mountains where, in a gully, he arranged his belongings, lay down, and died. The snow that covered his body turned to ice, trapping him in a glacier and preserving him to the present day.

Who was Ötzi?

Scientists have many ideas about who Ötzi was, where he came from, and what he was doing 10,496 ft. up in the ice-covered mountains. Most think he came from a village in northern Italy, in a valley at the foot of the Alps. He has been described as a shepherd, a hunter, a metalworker (because of his ax), and a priest (because of his tattoos). He may have known the mountains well and tried to use them as an escape route after he was attacked.

▼ After being frozen in ice for 5,300 years Ötzi's head and shoulders emerged when the glacier melted a bit. Later his body was freed by a mountain rescue team, and this photograph was taken.

SUMMARY OF CHAPTER 1: TWO WAYS TO MAKE A MUMMY

What are mummies?
Mummies are the preserved bodies of dead people and animals whose bodies have not rotted away. Their soft tissue, hair, and nails have survived—sometimes for thousands of years. Some mummies are accidents of nature, preserved by the movement of hot sand, dry air, or ice. Others are artificial mummies—ones that have been made on purpose by embalmers who found ways of stopping the bodies from rotting.

Who made mummies?
Mummy-making cultures have existed all over the world. The best known is that of ancient Egypt, where embalmers preserved almost anything from a peasant to a pharaoh, a cat to a crocodile. But they were not the first to make mummies—that claim to fame belongs to the Chinchorro people of Chile, who took bodies apart and then rebuilt them.

Why did people make mummies?
There are many reasons why mummies were made. For some people, such as the ancient Egyptians, there was a belief in life after death—but the promise of living forever in the afterlife was only possible if the person's body was preserved. If the body did not survive, the person could not be reborn into it—the person would be a "nobody." For other peoples the reason behind mummification was so they could keep the dead with them a little longer, treating them like they were still alive by talking to them and leaving food for them.

What is so special about natural mummies?
All mummies are special, but natural ones can provide us with information that artificial ones cannot. When we study an artificial mummy, we see only what the embalmers wanted us to see. But when we study a natural mummy, such as Ötzi the Iceman, we see a person at the moment of death, complete with the ordinary possessions they had with them. This gives us a close-up picture of that person's everyday life and the times they lived in.

Go further . . .

For an article written by experts who have studied the Chinchorro visit:
www.archaeology.org/online/features/Chinchorro

Visit the Discovery Channel's feature on Ötzi the Iceman at:
dsc.discovery.com/convergence/iceman/iceman.html

The Complete Book of Mummies by Claire Llewellyn (Hodder Wayland, 2001)

Secrets of the Ice Man by Dorothy Patent (Benchmark Books, 1998)

For older readers: *The Mummy Congress* by Heather Pringle (Fourth Estate, 2002)

Anthropologist
Studies the science of human beings and their way of life. By studying mummies anthropologists discover more about a people's way of life and can tell us how the mummy lived.

Archaeologist
Studies history by excavating sites—archaeologists are called to a site where mummies are found to record all findings.

Paleopathologist
Skilled in studying diseases of ancient people—paleopathologists carry out autopsies on mummies to find out about their health and cause of death.

Many museums display mummies—check in your local museum to see if there are any animal or human mummies on display.

Explore the Egyptian Museum at the Michael C. Carlos Museum at Emory University.
www.carlos.emory.edu
Michael C. Carlos Museum
Atlanta, GA 30322
Phone: (404) 727-4282

Visit Ötzi the Iceman at the South Tyrol Museum of Archaeology in Bolzano, Italy:
www.archaeologiemuseum.it

CHAPTER 2

Egypt, the land of mummies

Of all of the places where mummies were made, Egypt holds us in its spell more than any other. There, along the Nile river, embalmers worked in tents far from the towns and villages of the living. Their duty was to prepare the dead for the next stage of their lives. In ancient Egypt death was not the end of a person's life, instead it was a change from one level of existence to another. Death was a doorway through which everyone passed, from peasant to pharaoh. They hoped to be reborn on the other side, rising again to live forever in a perfect world. Meanwhile, in the imperfect world they had left behind, robbers unwrapped their bodies in search of treasures. But not all mummies were robbed. Many, such as Tutankhamen (below), escaped the robbers, and we can study them today, learning from them about the times in which they lived and died.

Why the Egyptians made mummies

The ancient Egyptians believed in life after death. To them death was simply the next stage in a person's life cycle. They believed that after death they traveled to the afterlife, where they were reborn and lived forever—but this could only take place if their bodies were preserved. It was for this reason that the Egyptians made mummies.

▲ The moment a person died, their *ba* left their body. Pictured as a bird with a human head, the *ba* was a spirit that represented the person's unique personality.

Egypt's natural mummies

Ancient Egypt's first mummies were made around 6,000 years ago, but they were not made by people. Instead they were accidents of nature created by the hot and dry conditions of Egypt's environment. When a body was buried, the hot, dry sand absorbed its moisture, and rather than rotting away, its soft tissue slowly dried out, creating a natural mummy.

Egypt's artificial mummies

Perhaps it was the unexpected discovery of sand-dried bodies—natural mummies—that first gave the Egyptians the idea of experimenting with ways of preserving human tissue. The first attempts at making mummies on purpose seem to have been made around 3400 B.C. As the craft of mummy making was perfected and spread throughout Egypt it became the accepted method of preparing a person for everlasting life, or immortality. To become an immortal was the next stage in a person's existence. Everyone wanted to be reborn and live forever in the afterlife, but for this to happen the Egyptians believed that their bodies had to be saved and not allowed to rot away. Mummies were made in Egypt for more than 3,000 years, and it was not only people who were mummified—animals were, too (see page 28). Egypt's last human mummies were made around A.D. 400.

▲ This painting is on a wall inside an Egyptian tomb. It shows a man and a woman who have reached the afterlife, or Field of Reeds. This was the place every Egyptian hoped to enter after they died, where they would live forever. The Field of Reeds was imagined as a place like Egypt but where giant crops grew, no one was hungry, and everyone was always happy.

The Egyptian afterlife

The Egyptians said death was the "night of going forth to life." It was their way of saying a person was about to begin the journey to a new existence in the afterlife. It was a difficult journey—with lakes of fire to cross and monsters to avoid. If the person said the right spells and passed a series of tests, they would enter the afterlife. If they failed, they would not become immortal.

The importance of the mummy

The Egyptians believed that they had a body and five nonphysical aspects. The major aspects were the *ba*, the *ka,* and the *akh* (similar to the idea of spirits or souls). After death the *ba* and *ka* took care of the person—but only if there was a mummy to visit. Without a mummy the person could not travel to the afterlife—where they would be reborn as their *akh*, which was the state of immortality.

◄ This man died in Egypt around 5,200 years ago. A pit was dug in the sand, and his body was carefully lowered into it. He was laid to rest on his side with his arms close to his chest, and his legs tucked under him. It looked as if he was asleep. After pots of food and drink were put beside him the burial pit was filled with sand. His body dried out slowly, and he became a natural mummy.

How the Egyptians made a mummy

Around 450 B.C. a Greek traveler visited Egypt. His name was Herodotus, and he wrote a book about Egypt's geography, customs, and history. For us, 2,500 years later, it is an important source of information, since Herodotus wrote the earliest known description of how the ancient Egyptians made mummies. Much of what Herodotus said has been shown to be true by modern science, helping us understand how the Egyptians transformed a body into a mummy. From beginning to end the body-preserving process took around 70 days.

The embalmers' workshops

Embalmers worked on the west bank of the Nile river. This was the side of the river associated with death and the afterlife because the sun set (died) in the west before rising (being reborn) to live again. Embalmers, who were always men, worked in open-air tents. In a tent called the "Place of Purification" (*ibu* in ancient Egyptian) the body was washed with a solution of natron (a mineral salt). This purified the body, leaving it ready for mummification to begin.

Clean—inside and out

After being washed the purified body was taken to the "House of Beauty" tent (*per-nefer* in ancient Egyptian), where it was placed on its back on a sloped table. The team of embalmers worked around the body, with each man doing a specific task. First the brain, which was not thought to be important, was removed—usually through the nose—and thrown away. Next the left side of the abdomen was cut open, and an embalmer removed the lungs, liver, intestines, and stomach with his bare hands. These organs were taken away to be individually mummified. The heart and kidneys were left in place.

Why the organs were removed

A body starts to decay from the moment of its death. In Egypt's hot climate this can be a rapid process, sped up by the work of meat-eating bacteria, maggots, worms, and beetles. The last thing the Egyptians wanted was for a body to be destroyed, since without it a person had no hope of being reborn. Because a body's organs are the first to rot, the Egyptians removed them from the corpse and so prevented the onset of decomposition.

▶ According to an ancient Greek traveler named Diodorus, to remove a body's organs one embalmer—a "scribe"—marked a cut line on the abdomen. The "slitter" cut along the line with a sharp stone knife, and the internal organs were removed. They were passed to the "pickler," whose job was to mummify them. The embalming table sloped from head to toe, which allowed fluids to drain into a container.

◀ Egyptian pictures show that one embalmer wore a mask that made him look like Anubis, a jackal-headed god. Anubis was the god of embalming. The embalmer who wore the Anubis mask was the chief embalmer, known as the "Master of Secrets."

Useless brain, useful heart

The Egyptians believed that the heart was the most important organ. They thought it was a person's "control center," and so it was left inside the body. The heart's beat was said to be its "voice." The Egyptians did not know that it is actually the brain that controls the body, which is why they considered it to be useless and threw it away.

▼ An embalmer may have used these bronze tweezers to dab the body with swabs of linen soaked in hot oil or resin. The swabs may have been too hot to touch, so tweezers would have avoided burned fingers.

▼ An embalmer inserted this bronze hook into the body's left nostril, pushed hard until it entered the skull, and then twisted it to break the brain down until it could be drained through the nose.

Drying and wrapping the body

After the organs had been removed the drying-out stage of the mummification process began. This usually started on the fifteenth day of the 70 days it took to make a mummy. To dry a body embalmers tried to remove as much moisture from it as possible, leaving it bone-dry and withered. The complete dehydration of a body took around 40 days. The final stage of making the mummy was wrapping the body in linen strips—a job that took 15 days.

▲ Spells from the Book of the Dead were written on a mummy's linen wrappings. The person's name was often written into the spells in order to protect them on the difficult journey to the afterlife.

▲ The embalmers' final duty was to place a mask over the head of the wrapped body. It was not meant to be a likeness of the person. Instead it showed how the person would like to look in the next life. While pharaohs' masks were made of gold, those of ordinary people were often made of cartonnage (linen stiffened with plaster).

Natron, the body-drying salt

Long before Egypt's embalmers mummified bodies fishermen had discovered how to salt fish, preserving it to eat later. They smothered their catch with a salt found on the shores of lakes. The Egyptians called it *neteryt*, which means "belonging to the god." We call it natron, named after the Wadi Natrun where it is found. Natron, a mixture mostly of sodium carbonate and sodium bicarbonate, is a desiccant—something that absorbs moisture. The knowledge that natron had the power to preserve flesh may have been passed on from fishermen to embalmers.

First wash, first packing, then salted

The body was cleansed inside and out with water and wine made from the fruit of date palm trees. Embalmers then packed the empty body cavity with bags of natron and rags and straw to give it a lifelike shape. It was then placed on a table and covered with dry natron—possibly as much as 500 lbs.—where it was left to dry out slowly.

▲ This linen bag contains natron. Bags, such as this one, were packed inside the body cavity, where the natron salt absorbed the body's fluids during the 40 days it took to dry it out.

A large amount of linen was used to wrap a body. The head and limbs were wrapped first and then the torso. Amulets were placed between the layers. A wrapped body was bulky, but it still retained the basic shape of a person. When the wrapping was over, the mummy was ready for burial.

▶ A plaque decorated with the Eye of Horus (the wedjat eye) was put over the cut in the abdomen. The amulet was thought to stop evil from entering the body.

Second wash, second packing, then oiled

After drying the body was dark and withered. Its limbs were like sticks, and it weighed one fourth of its original weight. The embalmers then began giving it a lifelike look. It was washed, and the used natron was taken from the body cavity, which was then repacked with linen, sawdust, and even mud. The skin was rubbed with oils and perfumes, and the body was covered with hot pine resin that set into a hard layer and stopped mold from attacking it.

Protected by charms and spells, wrapped from head to toe

False eyes were often put in the body's eye sockets, and a wig was put on its head. Charms, known as amulets, were placed on the body and among the linen strips that wrapped it from head to toe. Amulets saved the person from harm on their journey to the afterlife. Spells from the Book of the Dead were written on the wrappings or on a papyrus scroll. After wrapping resin was poured over the mummy to strengthen it and make it waterproof.

Coffins and canopics

When the embalmers had finished, the wrapped mummy was returned to its family, ready for burial. With it went the person's mummified organs (sometimes in special containers), together with the used packing materials and natron from the embalming process. Because these had touched the body, it was thought that they contained parts of the person. They were buried with the mummy to keep the person whole.

▲ A person's mummified organs were placed inside canopic jars such as these, each of which represented a minor god. From left to right the jars held the lungs, stomach, intestines, and liver.

A coffin to protect the body
The dead person's family provided the coffin, into which the mummy was placed. It was referred to as a "chest of life" and was thought of as a "house" for the *ka* (the person's life force or "identical twin" that was freed from their body at the time of death and that lived in the tomb). The coffin was often ornately decorated. Protective spells were written on it, and a "map" showed the route to the afterlife.

◀ Mummiform coffins—coffins shaped like a mummy—may have acted as "body doubles." If the real body was lost, perhaps its coffin would become a substitute for it so the person could still reach the afterlife.

Protecting the organs
The lungs, liver, intestines, and stomach were dried out using natron in the same way as the body was. When it was dry, each organ was wrapped. Sometimes the organs were put back inside the body. Other times they were put into containers known as canopic jars.

Buried in a tomb
The journey to the afterlife began on the day of burial. The coffin holding the mummy and the person's mummified organs were taken by the family to a cemetery. Outside the tomb a priest touched the mouth, ears, eyes, and nose of the mummy. This was the "Opening of the Mouth" ceremony, which restored the person's senses so that they would be able to eat, drink, hear, see, and smell again in their new life after death. The coffin was taken into a tomb, and goods for the person to use in the afterlife were left with it. The wealthy were buried with everything from food to furniture; the poor had much less. Then the tomb entrance was sealed, and the mummy was left to rest in peace— hopefully undisturbed by tomb robbers who searched for tombs to loot.

▼ An archaeologist examines a mummy and a group of decorated coffins discovered in the 1940s. A wrapped mummy was placed inside a wooden coffin, which was sometimes placed into several larger coffins for better protection.

Royal mummies

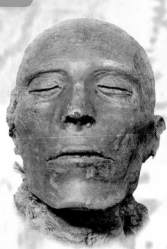

▲ Seti I was Egypt's pharaoh for 15 years—from 1294–1279 B.C. His mummy was buried in an ornately painted tomb in the Valley of the Kings. Seti's tomb was found in 1817, but his mummy was gone.

When a pharaoh died, his or her mummified body was buried along with hundreds of objects to use in the new life after death. While most burial objects were looted by robbers long ago, many mummies of Egypt's rulers have survived to the present day. The discoveries of royal mummies over the years have allowed us to look at the faces of ancient Egypt's pharoahs.

▲ The mummy of a woman, possibly Queen Tiye, who was married to pharaoh Amenhotep III (reigned 1390–1352 B.C.). A lock of her hair, found in the tomb of Tutankhamen, was used to identify the queen.

Pharaoh Seti I and the reburial of Egypt's kings

When Seti I's mummy was placed in its tomb—dug into the side of a valley south of Egypt, near the city of Thebes (present-day Luxor)—it was meant to rest in peace forever. However, robbers ransacked the tomb and disturbed his mummy. In their search for valuables they snapped the king's head off and ripped open his wrappings. Around 280 years after his death, approximately 1000 B.C., priests removed Seti's mummy from his tomb. They reburied it with a group, or cache, of around 40 others in a tomb nearby at Deir el-Bahari, where he lay undisturbed for almost 3,000 years.

▼ Ramses II was pharaoh for 66 years— from 1279–1213 B.C. He was the son of Seti I, and, like his father, he was first buried in the Valley of the Kings, then later reburied with other mummies after his tomb was robbed.

Pharaoh Ramses II and his peppery nose

On June 1, 1886 French archaeologist Gaston Maspero (1846–1916) removed the wrappings from the mummy of Ramses II. One of Egypt's greatest pharaohs, Ramses had died in his 90s after a very long reign. When the linen strips came off the old man's body, his mummy was found to be well preserved—especially his nose. A nose does not have bone in it, so it often ended up lost or squashed during mummification. However, when Ramses was X-rayed in the 1970s, his pointed nose was found to be filled with peppercorns, which had given it its distinctive shape. The X rays also revealed that Ramses had suffered from arthritis in his hips, and his teeth were full of holes—so he probably had bad breath, too.

A rushed job or a murder victim?

How the boy pharaoh Tutankhamen died is one of the great unsolved mysteries of ancient Egypt. X rays have revealed a tiny fragment of loose bone lodged deep inside his skull. Some people say it is evidence that the embalmers damaged the body in their haste to remove the king's brain. Others say he was murdered by a blow to the head.

Egypt's royal mummy caches

When Ahmed el-Rassul searched for his goat at Deir el-Bahari in 1871, he found it had fallen into a tomb. Inside were around 40 mummies, many of whom were Egypt's kings and queens. For ten years he secretly looted the tomb, but after an argument officials were led to it in 1881. All of the mummies were taken to Cairo Museum. A second cache of royal mummies was found in 1898.

▶ Aged between 18–20 when he died, the pharaoh Tutankhamen (reigned 1336–1327 B.C.) was buried in a small tomb in the Valley of the Kings. His mummy was very brittle and already in pieces when it was examined in 1925.

Nobles and commoners

Every Egyptian wanted their body preserved after they died in the hope of gaining everlasting life. This was the dream shared by both rich and poor. While the families of nobles had their loved ones expensively embalmed and buried in magnificent tombs, commoners were laid to rest in vast desert cemeteries. Everyone hoped to be reborn in the afterlife.

▲ Asru's mummy was unwrapped before it came to Manchester Museum in England in 1825. Today, almost 3,000 years after she was embalmed, resins used in the mummification can still be smelled on Asru's skin.

Asru, an elderly singer in an Egyptian temple

Women in ancient Egypt had short lives, with many not reaching 30 years old. Some, however, did grow old, such as Asru, who lived into her 60s. An inscription on her coffin tells us that she was a temple singer. An examination has revealed that her fingerprints were not overworked, showing she had not used her hands for hard labor. Instead she had probably enjoyed a comfortable lifestyle in the temple. However, this old lady was not in good health. Bad teeth gave her toothache, her fingers were stiff with arthritis, lung disease probably caused her to cough and left her breathless, and worms in her intestines would have made her weak.

King or commoner?

No one is certain about what happened to the mummy of pharaoh Tuthmosis I (reigned 1504–1492 B.C.), but 500 years after his death a priest may have been buried in his coffin. The coffin has the names of both the pharaoh and the priest on it—but the true identity of the mummy found inside is a mystery. It cannot be the priest, who died around 1032 B.C., because the mummy has been dated to around 1525 B.C. But this date is close to that of Tuthmosis' death—so could it be the king after all? The experts cannot agree. Perhaps one day DNA testing (see page 53) will explain this mystery.

Egypt's last mummies

Embalming was at its best in Egypt around 1000 B.C. This was when mummy makers attempted to restore a body's natural looks. Mummified organs were put back into the body cavity, skin was painted (red for men, yellow for women), and linen, sawdust, and mud filled out the person's shape. After 500 B.C. standards fell, and bodies were often badly preserved. Despite this, a lot of attention was paid to wrapping the body.

◄ This is the mummy found in the coffin of pharoah Tuthmosis I. Because there were no labels attached to the mummy's wrappings, the man's identity is not known. He could be a king or a commoner.

◄ The label attached to this mummy gave her name as Nodjmet. She was the wife of Herihor, a priest who ruled alongside the pharaoh, Ramses XI. Nodjmet died around 1069 B.C., and her embalmers made her mummy as lifelike as possible. Her body was painted with a skin-colored yellow, her mummified organs were put back in place, her cheeks were stuffed, and she was given stone eyes and a long wig.

▲ Mummies, such as this one, dating from the A.D. 100s, were among the last made in Egypt. Bodies were poorly mummified, but they were carefully wrapped and wore painted portrait masks.

An underground cemetery of golden mummies

In 1996 a donkey got its leg stuck in a hole at the Bahariya oasis, 248 mi. south of Cairo. Its owner freed it, widened the hole, and climbed down into an unknown tomb, where he found a mummy. It turned out to be the first of an estimated 10,000 mummies of ordinary people buried in 200 family tombs. They are 2,000 years old, and because many have gilded masks, the vast underground cemetery is now called the Valley of the Golden Mummies.

▲ An archaeologist working in the Valley of the Golden Mummies brushes sand away to reveal the gleaming mask of a mummy, one of thousands buried in the site's underground tombs. This series of tombs contains the largest collection of Egyptian mummies ever found in one place.

Animal mummies of Egypt

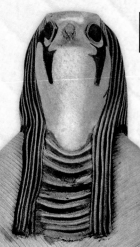

It was not only people that the embalmers of ancient Egypt made into mummies—they mummified animals, too. Some, such as flies and beetles, were attracted by the smell of decaying human flesh coming from the embalmers' workshops. When they settled on a mummy, they became trapped in the sticky resin that covered it and were embalmed by accident. But millions of other animals were made into mummies on purpose.

The purpose of animal mummies

Animal mummies were made for four reasons: as food for a person in the next life; so that pets could stay with their owners forever; as sacred animals that were worshiped; and as gifts to the gods. Food mummies took the form of pieces of meat and whole animals such as birds. Mummified pets included dogs, cats, and monkeys. Sacred bulls were mummified. Cats, birds, fish, and even snakes and eels were offered in this way as gifts to the gods.

How animal mummies were made

Embalmers made animal mummies in different ways depending on what the animals were. For example, a sacred bull was embalmed in the same way as a human. Its vital organs—except its heart—were removed, and its body was dried with natron (a mineral salt) and then packed to restore its shape before being wrapped. Other animals were treated more simply. Birds were dipped whole in molten resin and then wrapped. Fish were gutted, dried, and wrapped.

◄ The carefully wrapped mummy of a falcon. Some birds-of-prey mummies had human-face masks, and it was once thought they were mummies of children—until they were unwrapped or X-rayed.

▼ The mummy of an embalmed crocodile. Crocodiles were worshiped and kept in sacred pools. All sizes of crocodiles were mummified—sometimes together with clutches of eggs.

► Mummy of a dog, or more likely—because of its black face—a jackal. Jackals were associated with death because they lived close to cemeteries. However, black was also thought of as the color of life because new plants grew out of Egypt's black soil along the Nile river.

Burial grounds for animals

In the same way that mummified humans were buried in cemeteries, animals were, too. Different species even had their own cemeteries. There were huge cat cemeteries 50 mi. northeast of Cairo at Bubastis—the religious center of the cat goddess Bastet. Part of the massive human cemetery at Saqqâra, 12 mi. south of Cairo, was set aside for animals. Millions of ibis, baboons, hawks, jackals, cats, and dogs were buried there, as well as the sacred Apis bulls, in a series of subterranean chambers, or catacombs.

► Cats were not just pets—they worked as bird scarers and protected crops from mice. Many were killed and then embalmed. After wrapping their features were painted or sewn on.

Egypt's sacred bulls and the Serapeum at Saqqâra

The most sacred animal was the Apis bull, which was chosen for its markings, especially the diamond shape on its forehead. It was thought to contain the spirit of one of the creator gods, Ptah. The bull lived for around 15 years. After death it was mummified and buried in a granite sarcophagus in catacombs, known as the Serapeum, at Saqqâra. A new Apis bull was then chosen, and the cycle began again.

Did animals enjoy a life after death?

Unlike people, for whom death was thought of as the next stage in their lives, most animals were not expected to be reborn in the afterlife. For them death really was the end of their lives. However, animals, such as sacred Apis bulls and pampered pets, that were given the full mummification process were believed to live a new life after death. Like people, they too became immortal.

◄ This mummified bull or calf, intricately wrapped in linen, was made around 30 B.C. It has colored linen patches on its eyes and a shaped piece of linen on its forehead, perhaps to link it to the sacred Apis bull.

▼ Snakes were regarded as sacred to another creator god, Atum, as well as other gods. They were killed and mummified and placed inside of boxes such as this one.

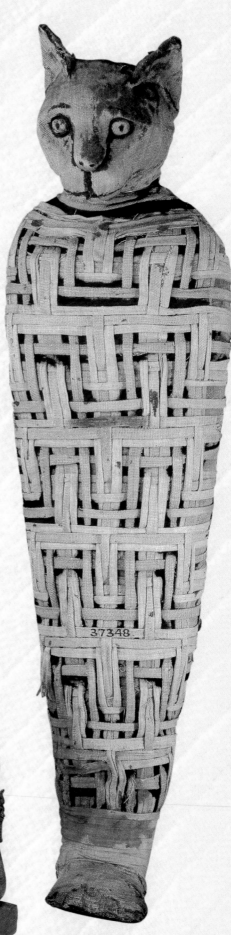

SUMMARY OF CHAPTER 2: EGYPT, THE LAND OF MUMMIES

Why did the ancient Egyptians make mummies?
Because the ancient Egyptians believed in life after death, they thought it was essential to stop a person's body from rotting away. If the body decayed, the person would not live again in the afterlife. Egypt's first mummies were those that dried out naturally in the hot desert sand. When embalmers discovered that natron salt could be used to dry out a body, they started using it to preserve the dead, who became artificial mummies.

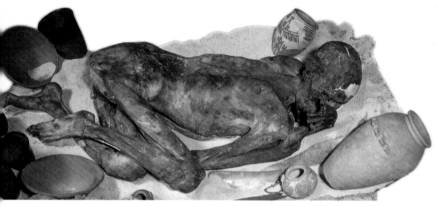

How long did it take to make a mummy?
The Greek historian Herodotus, who is known as the "Father of History," described in a book how the Egyptians made mummies. He said the mummification process took 70 days. In the first 15 days after death the body was taken to the embalmers' workshops, where it was cleansed and purified, and its organs were removed. For the next 40 days it laid under a pile of body-drying natron. During the final 15 days its shape was restored with stuffing materials, its skin was oiled, and it was wrapped in strips of linen. The mummy was then ready for burial.

Why did the ancient Egyptians mummify animals?
Millions of animals were mummified in ancient Egypt. Some were mummified because they were family pets. Their mummies were placed in their owners' tombs so they would be with them in the afterlife. Other animals—or parts of animals—were mummified to provide food for a dead person. Some were sacrifices to please the gods, while others were sacred animals that were worshiped in their own temples.

Go further . . .

For the British Museum on ancient Egyptian mummies:
www.ancientegypt.co.uk

National Geographic site on "How to make a mummy" is at:
www.nationalgeographic.com/media/tv/mummy/index.html

For news of mummy discoveries in Egypt and the official web site of Dr. Zahi Hawass, whose team excavated the Valley of the Golden Mummies, visit: www.guardians.net/hawass/

The Royal Mummies by Eric Kudalis (Capstone, 2002)

Lift the Lid: Mummies by Saul Arlosoroff (Apple Press, 2000)

Egyptologist
Specializes in the history of the ancient Egyptians through archaeological excavations, studies, etc.

Embalmer
Someone who prepares the body of a dead person so that it is ready for a funeral.

Epigraphist
Skilled in studying inscriptions on tombs and inscribing stones. An epigraphist makes sense of inscriptions.

The Egyptian Museum in Cairo, Egypt, houses many Egyptian mummies, including Ramses II:
www.touregypt.net/egyptmuseum/egyptian_museum.htm
The Egyptian Museum
Tahrir Square
Cairo, Egypt

The Brooklyn Museum in New York City has a collection of Egyptian art, mummy cases, and two mummies:
www.brooklynmuseum.org
The Brooklyn Museum
Brooklyn, NY 11238
Phone: (718) 638-5000

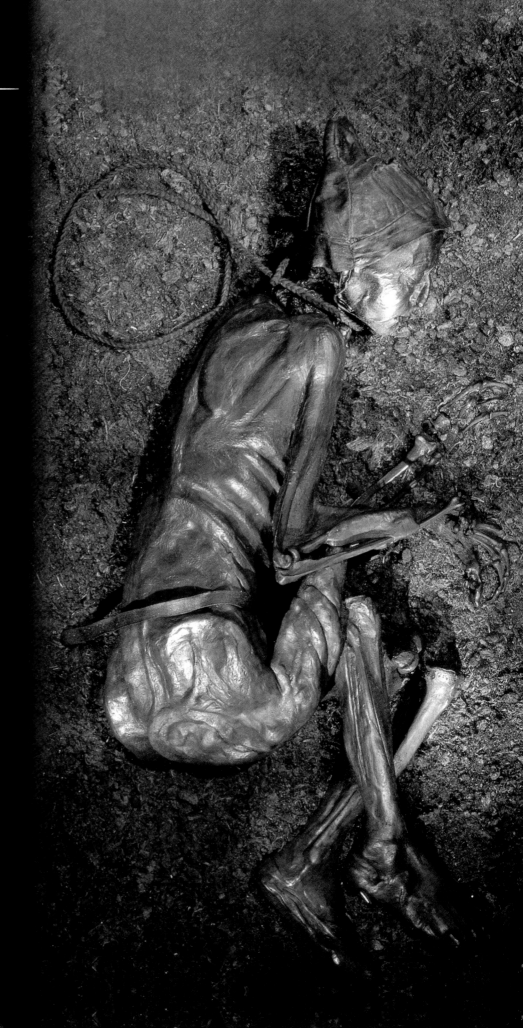

CHAPTER 3

Mummy world

We live in a world full of mummies, but the worlds they knew vanished long ago. While their preserved bodies rested in tombs of desert sand, frozen ground, watery peat, and dry air, time has passed them by. The continents have crept across Earth, ice ages have come and gone, civilizations have blossomed and withered, and explorers have charted the land and the seas. History has been made, and all the time these mummies have been its silent witnesses, waiting for the day when they can return to the land of the living and tell their stories. We are their guardians—the ones who find them, the ones who save them from turning into dust, and the ones who ask questions that their long-dead bodies can answer. They are time capsules.

Tollund Man (see pages 32–33)

Bog bodies of Europe

The cold, wet peat bogs of northern Europe are ideal places for the natural preservation of skin and bone, as well as hair and flesh. More than 2,000 ancient bodies have been pulled out from bogs in Denmark, Germany, the Netherlands, Ireland, and Great Britain. Most date from 500 B.C.–A.D. 500. How and why people ended up in such dark, watery places tells us more about prehistoric Europe.

▲ Windeby Girl, from northern Germany, was around 14 when she died. Around A.D. 100 she went blindfolded and naked to a small bog, where it seems she drowned. Her body was lowered into the bog, and a large stone and branches were used to weight it down.

Peat's preserving powers

Peat is formed from plants that have partially rotted in water. As the layers of plants build up those at the bottom are squashed into a dense, spongy mass of peat. Bogs made of sphagnum moss have special properties. As it turns into peat the moss releases chemicals that destroy body-rotting bacteria and preserve the skin. There is little oxygen in a peat bog and no flesh-eating creatures. It is a perfect place to preserve a body.

▼ Denmark's Tollund Man is Europe's most famous bog body. He has kept this peaceful, sleeplike pose for 2,100 years, ever since he was hanged by his neck until dead.

Why are there bodies in the bogs?

Some bog bodies may be the result of accidents, where people fell in and drowned. Most people, however, were deliberately put into the bogs. Many show signs of having met violent deaths. Their throats are cut or bound with suffocating cords. Wooden stakes pinned some to the ground—they were not meant to escape. To the people of prehistoric Europe watery places held special interest. Objects were placed in rivers and lakes, perhaps as gifts to the gods. The greatest gift of all may have been a human life. So Europe's bog bodies may be the victims of religious sacrifices. As they disappeared from the world of the living these people entered the world of the gods. Or, perhaps, they may be executed criminals or murder victims.

▶ Lindow Man, from a marsh in Cheshire, England, died around A.D. 100. He was hit on the head, strangled, and his throat was cut. Mistletoe pollen was found in his stomach—perhaps this 20-year-old man ate a sacred meal before his life was sacrificed.

Tollund Man's last meal

In May 1950 peat cutters in Tollund Fen, Denmark, uncovered a man's well-preserved body nine feet below ground level. He was around 45 when he met his death at the end of a hangman's leather noose around 100 B.C. His body—naked except for a cap and a belt—was buried in the bog, placed on its side with its legs tucked up, as if asleep. Inside his intestines were the remains of his last meal—a barley porridge.

Keeping bog bodies safe for the future

As soon as a bog body is exposed to the air time catches up with it, and the natural process of decay begins. In 1950 only the head of Tollund Man could be saved (it is now joined to a model of the original body). By 1984, when Lindow Man was found, it was possible to preserve a complete body.

▶ After being entombed in deep peat for centuries a body usually becomes wrinkled and flattened such as this one. Found by peat cutters in Denmark in 1892, this was the first bog body to be photographed.

Mummies of Italy and Sicily

Christian churches and cathedrals are the usual resting places of the dead. Graves of commoners fill cemeteries outside, while the mortal remains of the wealthy and famous are kept inside. In Italy and Sicily many bodies lie intact. Their mummified corpses—or parts of them—are put on display.

▲ Inside this bag are relics—body parts—of St. John of Capestrano (1386–1456) in Italy. In the Middle Ages pieces from a holy person's body were often sent to different churches, where they were displayed for the faithful to see and worship.

Mummies of the incorruptible saints

Before a person becomes a saint the Roman Catholic church investigates his or her life. Many factors are taken into account, one of which is whether the person's body has been preserved. If it has, it is seen as a miracle. Saints whose bodies were preserved are known as "incorruptibles"—time has not corrupted (rotted) them. In Italy there are mummies of around 25 saints who died between the A.D. 300s and 1400s. Most were preserved by natural processes, but some were preserved on purpose.

St. Margaret of Cortona—the mummy that time forgot

The cathedral in Cortona, Italy, displays the mummy of St. Margaret (1247–1297), patron saint of midwives. In her lifetime it was said she worked miracles. When she died, the faithful of Cortona preserved her body so they could continue to ask for her blessings. As the years passed this fact was forgotten, and she was seen as an incorruptible. Only in 1988, when her mummy was examined, were the cuts and stitches of the medieval embalmers revealed.

Sicily's catacomb corpses

Sicily, a large island south of Italy, has a bone-dry climate. It is ideal for the preservation of bodies, drying them out slowly until they become natural mummies. In a catacomb beneath a church in Palermo are 8,000 of these human remnants. Some grin from open coffins; others stare out from openings in the walls. Many stand on stiff legs, with their heads at strange angles. The oldest has been there 400 years, the youngest less than a century.

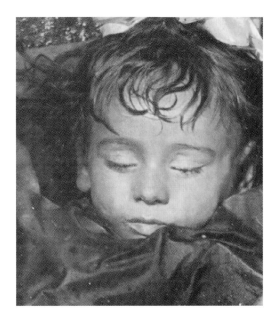

▲ Rosalia Lombardo died in 1920, aged two. Her father, a doctor, preserved her body. She was one of the last Sicilians to be mummified.

Roman girl is a mummy

The Romans are not known as mummy makers, yet in 1964 the mummy of an eight-year-old girl was discovered in Grottarossa on the northern outskirts of Rome, Italy. She had died around A.D.175 and had been buried in a marble sarcophagus. When the lid was lifted, her body was still lifelike, but contact with the air soon caused it to wrinkle and turn dark brown. A Roman embalmer had preserved her with oils and resins.

◄ As if rising up from the dead, the dried-out bodies of men, women, and children, dressed in their best clothes, line the walls of a catacomb under a church in Palermo, Sicily.

▲ St. Rita of Cascia (1381–1457) in Italy is the saint of lost causes. She is known as the "Saint of the Impossible." Her embalmed body is said to give off a sweet scent.

North America and Greenland

The deliberate embalming of bodies was not practiced by the native people of North America and Greenland. Despite this, mummies do exist. They have become naturally preserved because of environmental conditions. Bodies entombed in Arctic ice can look hauntingly alive, and the hot, dry deserts to the south have dried others into wrinkled husks.

▶ In Guanajuato, a town high up in the mountains of Mexico, the dead are laid to rest in crypts. Their bodies slowly dry out until they become natural mummies, like the baby seen here. Some are displayed in the town's museum.

The mummies of Qilakitsoq

In 1972 hunters in Greenland discovered the mummified bodies of eight Inuit people. They found two graves—one with five bodies, the other with three. These native Greenlanders—six women and two children—had died around 1475 in Qilakitsoq on the island's west coast. Buried on a rock ledge inside the Arctic Circle, years of cold, dry air had freeze-dried the bodies. The women had died between the ages of 20 and 50. One child was about four years old, and the other was a baby. Perhaps they were three generations of a family—grandmother, mother, and child. These natural mummies give us an insight into the world of the Inuit of 500 years ago. They wore clothes made of sealskin—the perfect material for Arctic life. The adults had worn-down teeth, perhaps from chewing on sealskin to soften it to make clothing.

◀ The mummified body of a six-month-old Inuit from Greenland. The baby, who may be a boy, died around 1475 and was buried in warm, waterproof sealskin clothes. Because he is so small, his finders at first thought he was a doll.

Ice mummies of English explorers in Canada

In May 1845 the ships *Erebus* and *Terror* sailed from London, England. Onboard were 128 men, led by Sir John Franklin. The mission was to search for the Northwest Passage— a sea route across the Arctic Ocean that was thought to be a shortcut between the Atlantic and Pacific oceans. The expedition ended in tragedy, and all of the men died. In 1850 three graves were found in the Canadian Arctic, together with empty tin cans in which the Victorian explorers had carried their food. It was these cans that led to many of the men's deaths, although no one knew that at the time.

In 1984 the bodies of John Torrington, John Hartnell, and William Braine were exhumed from their icy graves. Each body was remarkably well-preserved by the Arctic ice, like meat in a freezer. Examination of the men revealed that they had high levels of poisonous lead in their bodies—enough to make them sick and weak. Lead from the seams on the cans had contaminated the food they had eaten. After examination each body was returned to its Arctic grave, where it lies today, deep-frozen again.

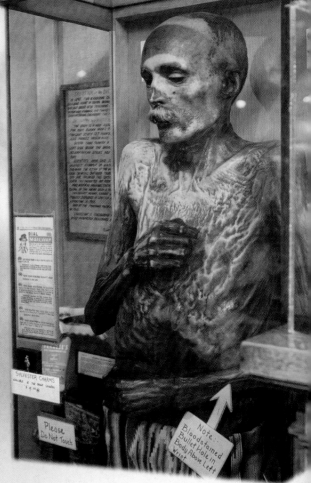

▶ This is the mummified body of "Sylvester." He has been on display in the Ye Olde Curiosity Shop in Seattle, Washington, since 1955. The man, whose real name is not known, was around 45 when he was shot and killed in the 1800s. He was found in 1895, buried in a sandy desert in Arizona. The hot, dry desert had dried out his body.

◀ John Torrington, aged 20, was buried in the icy ground of Beechey Island in the Canadian Arctic in 1846. He lay there, frozen stiff inside a block of ice, until his coffin was opened in 1984. Time had stopped, and he had not rotted away.

Native North American mummies

Many mummies have been found in the United States, particularly in Arizona, Tennessee, and Kentucky. There dry air and desert conditions have preserved organic material, including the bodies of native peoples buried in rock shelters and caves. They have dried out and become natural mummies. Most are around 1,500 years old. However, the body of a man from Spirit Cave in Nevada is a staggering 9,000 years old— North America's oldest mummy.

The "North American Iceman"

Hunters in British Columbia, Canada discovered the frozen body of a man in 1999. Because his headless corpse was found in a glacier, he has been compared with Ötzi, the ice mummy from Europe (see pages 12–13). He is known as the North American Iceman and also as Kwaday Dan Sinchi ("Long Ago Man" in the language of the tribal people on whose land he was found). Aged around 20, he had died in the first half of the 1400s, making his mummy around 575 years old. He wore a cloak made from Arctic squirrel skin and carried a walking stick, a spear, and a food pouch. After examination the mummy was handed over to the tribespeople, who claimed it as the body of an ancestor. It was cremated, and the ashes were buried close to where the mummy had been found.

South American mummies

Mummies were made in South America for 6,500 years— longer than anywhere else in the world. Not only is the continent the birthplace of mummy making, but it is also one of the last places where mummies were made deliberately, and some of them were paraded through the streets. Natural and artificial mummies belonging to different groups of people are found here.

Fourth layer— brightly colored, patterned cloth

▲ This "mummy bundle" from Peru was made around A.D. 800. The body was placed upright in a squatting position and then wrapped in layers of fabric. Grass and reeds were used for padding. A fake head was put on top of the bundle.

▼ This ten-year-old Inca girl, called Sarita, was a sacrifice to her gods 500 years ago. She died in her sleep high up on a mountain, where the dry and cold conditions preserved her body.

The right environment for natural mummies

The environment of South America has created many natural mummies. Along the coasts of Peru and Chile, where the temperature is hot and dry all year-round, bodies slowly dried out, leaving leathery skin stretched tightly over bones. High up in the mountains of Peru, where it is dry and always freezing cold, bodies do not decay. Instead they become deep-frozen and are preserved in every detail, both inside and out.

Mummies made on purpose

Not much is known about the methods used in South America to make artificial mummies. The Chinchorro culture (see pages 10–11) in Chile "rebuilt" the bodies of their dead around 5,000 B.C. There is then a long gap in our knowledge until the A.D. 1400s, when people in Bolivia and Peru eviscerated (gutted) their dead. They removed internal organs and even skin from bones. Resin was rubbed over the body, and it was prepared for burial.

▶ As early as the 400s B.C. people in southern Peru were making "mummy bundles," a practice that lasted for more than 1,000 years. The goal was to preserve a body by natural means. The organs were left inside the body, its knees were folded against its chest, and then it was bound with ropes and layers of fabric to produce a compact bundle. Over time body fluids were absorbed by the fabric, and the body dried out.

Rope was bound around the wrists and ankles

Children sacrificed to the gods

The Incas, who ruled much of South America between c.1200 and 1533, sacrificed children to their gods. Their young victims, known as *capacocha*, were chosen because they were young and healthy—only the best was good enough for the gods. Children were gifts to the gods, and in return the Incas hoped to be given rain for their crops, freedom from disease, and prosperity. Around 500 years ago, a teenage Inca girl was chosen to be a *capacocha*. On the icy summit of Mount Ampato in Peru she was killed. She may have been hit on the head or drugged and left to die of cold as she slept 20,664 ft. up on the mountain. Her frozen body, found in 1995, is almost perfectly preserved. She has been called Juanita.

Objects, such as feathers, were placed between the final layers

Third layer—plain cotton cloth

Second layer—colored, patterned cloth

▲ Juanita, "Ice Maiden of the Andes," is carried from her tomb. Wrapped in textiles, she had been buried with gold and silver statuettes, clay pots, and bags of corn. Inca children were sacrificed to the gods when a new emperor was crowned.

The "living corpses" of Peru

The Incas mummified the bodies of their dead emperors, but not one exists today—and it is not known how they were made. Royal mummies were displayed at festivals, where they were carried through the streets of Cuzco, the capital. The idea was to show them off as "living corpses." A mummy was proof of an emperor's existence, both in the past and in the present. The Spanish, who defeated the Incas in the 1530s, could not understand why people kept the preserved remains of their ancestors, tending to them as if they were still alive. To the Christian Spanish this was a pagan practice, and they began destroying Peru's mummies. In just four years 1,365 Inca mummies were found and destroyed.

First layer—plain cotton cloth

Body was placed on a thick cotton pad inside a basket

Food offering of corn

Mummies of Asia

The huge continent of Asia is the burial ground of many natural and artificial mummies, where bodies have been preserved by the contrasting effects of ice and fire, liquid and sand. It is the place where the West meets the East—where human bodies provide valuable clues that long-distance contact once existed but has since been long forgotten. The mummies of Asia are rewriting history.

► This mummy of a three-month-old baby wrapped in swaddling clothes was found in China's remote Taklimakan—a name that means "the desert of no return." The infant died around 1000 B.C. and lay in its dry tomb of sand for 3,000 years before being discovered.

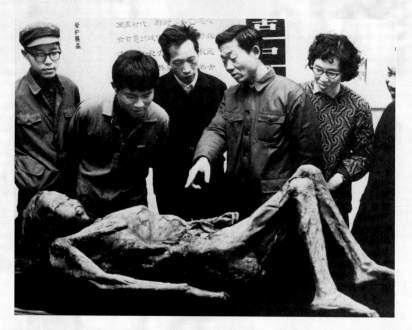

◄ Many natural and artificial mummies have been found in China. Some are so well preserved that hundreds of years after their death their arms and legs are as flexible as when they had just died.

A mummy made by mercury

One of the world's best-preserved mummies was found in China in 1972. She is Lady Ch'eng, and she died 2,100 years ago. The care taken over her burial was the cause of her preservation. Her body was laid inside a coffin that was filled with a mysterious liquid containing mercury. The coffin was sealed and placed inside another coffin and then another. The nest of coffins was buried under a mound of charcoal and clay. In this watertight, airtight tomb her body was preserved, seemingly aided by the mercury in which she lay for so long.

Mummies of the Chinese desert

The Taklimakan desert is in northwest China. Its minimal rainfall and salty sand mean that human bodies do not rot away. Here lies a mystery, not about how the desert's 3,000-year-old mummies were made but about where the people came from. It is a puzzle that is changing the way we think about the early history of China—for these people look European (fair hair, light skin, long bodies), not Asian (dark hair, dark skin, short bodies). Until the 1980s it was believed China had had no contact with the West before 150 B.C. The desert mummies show that the true date is much earlier.

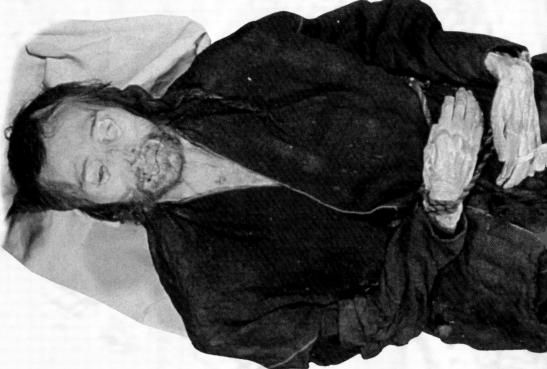

The mummy statue of Vietnam

Around A.D. 639 a remarkable thing is said to have happened to the body of a Buddhist monk at a shrine near Hanoi, Vietnam. The monk was Vu Khac Minh, and as his long life drew to an end he locked himself in his room to meditate . . . and die. He asked that no one enter the room for 100 days. When the time was up, instead of a maggot-eaten corpse, monks found that Vu Khac Minh's body was in perfect condition. He had died sitting cross-legged (a position of prayer). It was thought he had reached nirvana—the Buddhist state of perfect happiness. Monks coated his body in red lacquer and put it on display for all to observe.

◄ Vu Khac Minh was the Buddhist monk who was said to have been preserved through prayer alone. In fact, his body was dried out in soil and sawdust and then coated with resin mixed with silver.

▲ Tucked up inside painted wooden coffins are the mummified bodies of leaders of the Ibaloi tribe from Kabayan in the Philippines. They died around 500 years ago, and their bodies were slowly dried out over fires before being buried inside caves.

Ice mummies of Siberia

Herodotus, who described how the Egyptians made mummies (see page 18), also wrote about other mummy makers. He said the Scythians (ancient nomadic people from southern Siberia in the area bordering China and Mongolia) preserved their dead with spices. One group, the Pazyryk, lived in the Altai mountains. When a leading Pazyryk died, he or she was buried in a log-lined pit dug into the frozen ground. The icy tomb, called a kurgan, was covered with a mound of soil. Russians opened up some of the kurgans in the 1920s, but it was in 1993 that the most amazing find was made—when the 2,500-year-old deep-frozen mummy of a woman was found. Known as the "Ice Princess," her skin was tattooed with images of deer—an animal the Pazyryk hunted.

▲ Cherchen Man's mummified body was found in China's Taklimakan desert. The man, who died 3,000 years ago, has the features of a European rather than those of a Chinese person. It is evidence of ancient contact between the West and the East.

Mummies of the South Pacific

In the South Pacific the native peoples made mummies so that the dead could stay with the living awhile longer. However, it is one of the regions where questions about how we should respect the dead are being asked—these are questions for the whole world to consider.

Mummies of New Guinea and the Torres Strait

New Guinea is a large island north of Australia. Between the two islands is the Torres Strait. The area's people have a long history of preserving humans. Some were preserved so that the dead could stay with their families; others because they were leaders or warriors—the living wanted their power to continue protecting them. On Darnley Island in the Torres Strait the dead had their brains and internal organs taken out and their bodies stuffed with fibers from palm trees. They were then stretched over wooden frames and left to dry, after which time their families took them home.

▼ In the Asaro Caves of Papua New Guinea (the eastern part of the island of New Guinea) the stick-thin mummies of warriors killed in battle and village elders sit on wooden scaffolding. These natural, air-dried mummies are around 300 years old.

◄ This mummy is from West Irian, or Irian Jaya (the western part of the island of New Guinea). The dead person was placed into a squatting position, and the body was put into a tree, where it was left to dry out in the sun. Some were suspended from wooden beams and smoke-dried over fires—the same way that meat was dried so that it could be kept longer.

Mummies of Australia and respect for ancestors

Mummies were once made by the indigenous peoples (aborigines) of Australia. However, the preserved bodies of the continent's original inhabitants have barely been studied. It is known that they were made by drying out in the sun on tree platforms or over fires, but as with North American mummies (see page 37), there are reasons why scientists have not examined them. Australian museums have removed these mummies from their displays, and their pictures are rarely printed in books (there are none in this book). Some mummies have been handed back to aborigines who claim them as their ancestors.

This attitude is in contrast to how we treat mummies from other cultures, which are sometimes simply seen as objects. It is easy to forget that mummies were once living human beings. The descendants of the mummies of Australia want to make sure that we do not forget this. They want their ancestors to be respected and treated with dignity. For this reason science does not want to offend the living.

A price on the heads of the Maori of New Zealand

The Maori of New Zealand used to tattoo the faces of warriors and chiefs. The designs were meant to protect the wearer and scare away the enemy. But who was the real enemy of the Maori? In the 1800s European sailors traded weapons in exchange for Maori heads. The Maori obliged by tattooing prisoners, chopping off their heads, and trading them for guns. The trade was banned in 1831, by which time "trophy heads" had been taken to Europe and the Americas. In 1988 a British auction house was banned from selling a Maori head. The Maori Council said the sale was "a degrading and deeply offensive desecration." They claimed that the head was a cultural and spiritual artifact and should be returned to New Zealand for burial. Many have been returned, but around 200 are still in the hands of collectors.

Dinosaurs, mammoths, cats, and rats

▼ The mummy of the mammoth calf Dima was named after the stream in Siberia close to where he was found. The one-year-old baby died 40,000 years ago, possibly after getting trapped in mud. He was 35 in. tall and 43 in. long and was originally covered in long, red hair, which now only survives on his feet.

Anything is possible in the bizarre world of mummies—a dinosaur whose reptile skin imprint still covers its bones like a shroud; a mammoth whose body is so well preserved that it looks like it died yesterday, not in a time when humans hunted it for food. These ancient mummies reveal unique information about their species and the world in which they lived. But there are also animal mummies from the more recent past that reveal a superstitious side to human nature.

Fossil hunter finds a dinosaur mummy

In 1908 American fossil hunter Charles Sternberg made one of the greatest dinosaur finds ever—the 65-million-year-old mummy of an *Edmontosaurus*. He uncovered its fossilized body close to the town of Lusk, Wyoming. After it died the dinosaur's body had dried in the sun. Its internal organs had shrunk, and its skin had hardened over its bones, turning it into a natural mummy. Eventually it was buried under sand in a river, and the long process of turning bone into stone began. The *Edmontosaurus* became a fossil. An imprint of its bones and skin formed in the rock that entombed it, preserving every skin-wrinkled detail.

▼ This *Edmontosaurus* dinosaur died on its back with its right front arm in the air. You can see how its mummified skin is stretched over its rib cage. Its head, hind limbs, and tail did not survive—they were worn away by erosion long before the "mummy" was found.

Woolly mammoths of the Siberian tundra

Perhaps the most remarkable of all natural animal mummies are the
woolly mammoths discovered in the permanently frozen ground of Siberia.
These hairy elephantlike creatures, some with ivory tusks, lived during the last
great ice age (around 100,000 to 10,000 years ago). The species only became
extinct around 4,000 years ago—around the time Egypt's mummy makers
were searching for a way to preserve flesh. What if they
had known about the body-preserving power
of ice? Far to the north of their hot land
lay the deep-frozen giant bodies of
mammoths, already ancient when
the pyramids were built.

▲ This cat was closed up inside of a wall while still alive
in a house in Great Britain and left to die of starvation. This
ancient custom was believed to protect a house from harmful
spirits, which the cat would catch.

Dima, the mammoth that came in from the cold

When gold miner Alexei Logachev's bulldozer pushed
back frozen ground in Kirgilyak Creek in eastern Siberia,
he struck it rich. Since 1860 the Russian Academy of
Sciences had offered a reward to anyone who found
and reported a mammoth carcass—but no one had
ever done so. That all changed in 1977 when Logachev
uncovered a baby mammoth. It was given the name
Dima. Logachev received 1,000 rubles and a silver
medal, and science received the frozen body of the
best-preserved mammoth ever found so far. Dima
was flown to Leningrad, where his ancient body
was embalmed to prevent it from rotting. The
discovery made world headlines, and ever since
then Dima has been exhibited in Europe, North
America, and Japan. For insurance purposes this
unique prehistoric animal mummy has been valued
at an impressive $12 million. What price would you
expect for a human mummy (see page 58)?

Animal mummies and superstitions

Mummified animals can be found in old buildings.
There are dried-out bodies of trapped birds in attics,
rodents under floorboards, insects in roofs, and cats,
which have used up all of their nine lives, may be
found behind walls. In the U.S. we are superstitious
about black cats—they represent bad luck. In Great
Britain the opposite is true. In the 1600s and
1700s superstitious Britons bricked
them up behind walls to protect
their homes from evil.

▶ This 300-year-old brown rat once scurried
around the roof timbers of St. Thomas's Church
in Salisbury, England. There it died, and in the dusty,
dry air of the attic its body dried and mummified.

SUMMARY OF CHAPTER 3: MUMMY WORLD

Where are mummies found?

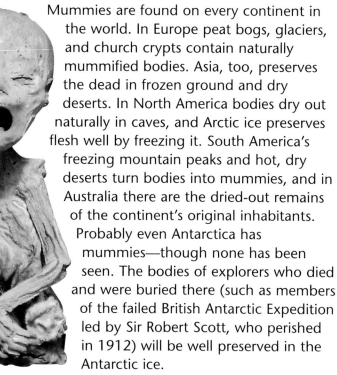

Mummies are found on every continent in the world. In Europe peat bogs, glaciers, and church crypts contain naturally mummified bodies. Asia, too, preserves the dead in frozen ground and dry deserts. In North America bodies dry out naturally in caves, and Arctic ice preserves flesh well by freezing it. South America's freezing mountain peaks and hot, dry deserts turn bodies into mummies, and in Australia there are the dried-out remains of the continent's original inhabitants. Probably even Antarctica has mummies—though none has been seen. The bodies of explorers who died and were buried there (such as members of the failed British Antarctic Expedition led by Sir Robert Scott, who perished in 1912) will be well preserved in the Antarctic ice.

Which is the oldest animal mummy?

Long before humans evolved dinosaurs ruled Earth. The mummified remains of one of these 65-million-year-old reptiles have been found, making it the oldest animal mummy found . . . so far.

Who do mummies belong to?

It might seem strange—even distasteful—to think of "owning" a mummy, especially if the mummy is a human body. The question of "ownership" is highly sensitive, but it needs to be asked. Mummies are more than "cultural property" such as carved stones removed from old buildings (like the ancient Greek Parthenon in Athens) or bronze figures looted by a conquering army (such as those taken by the British from Benin in west Africa). Mummies cannot speak, but their descendants now speak up for them, demanding that the bodies of their ancestors should be treated with dignity and not like laboratory animals. Out of respect for the dead and the wishes of the living mummies of the native peoples of North America and Australia have been returned to their descendants.

Go further . . .

A very good web site about mummies and mummification all over the world is:
www.mummytombs.com

For Discovery Channel features on mummies visit: dsc.discovery.com/convergence/mummies/mummies.html

For links to over 200 mummy web sites visit: www.mysteries-megasite.com/main/bigsearch/mummy-1.html

BBC History Online features mummies at: www.bbc.co.uk/history/ancient/egyptians/mummies_01.shtm

For older readers:
The Encyclopedia of Mummies by Dr. Bob Brier (Checkmark Books, 1998)

Curator
In charge of a museum area, ensuring the exhibits are kept in an environment that will keep them safe and in good condition.

Historian
Specializes in history, possibly within one area or country—studying mummies could be part of this chosen area.

Researcher
Studies a specific area, such as a type of mummy, and advises archaeologists, etc.

Museo de las Momias in Guanajuato, Mexico, houses over 100 natural mummies

In Silkeborg, Denmark visit the Silkeborg Museum to see Tollund Man:
www.silkeborgmuseum.dk/english/

Xinjiang Regional Museum in Ürümchi, China, houses the Cherchen mummies

Some Chinchorro mummies and artifacts are on display at the Archaelogy Museum of San Miguel de Azapa at the University of Tarapacá, Chile

CHAPTER 4

Mummies today

For centuries doctors in Europe used the ground-up bodies of Egyptian mummies in their medicines, believing that the ancient dust cured all illnesses. Until the 1900s a brown paint used by artists was made from— you guessed it—crushed mummies, and farmers fertilized their fields with the powder, growing crops that fed the people of Victorian England. Fortunately, the treatment of mummies has moved on since then. Today they are probed by scientists whose work unlocks facts about the past. And, of course, mummies mean movies to film studios, whose blockbusters fill movie theaters around the world. But there is more to mummies today than museum displays and big-screen thrills— there is also mummification itself, which is available to you—if you want it. Do you?

Movie actor
Boris Karloff
in *The Mummy*
(see page 50)

Modern mummies

If you think mummy making is dead, think again. There are embalmers working today, using a mixture of traditional methods and new technology to keep the ancient craft alive. The bodies of world leaders have been embalmed and publicly displayed, and even ordinary people can end up being mummified in the name of science and, believe it or not, art and entertainment.

Preserving an American president

One president of the U.S. has been mummified. The body of President Abraham Lincoln, who was assassinated in 1865, had its organs removed, its blood drained, and was then pumped with embalming fluids until it became as hard as stone. Why? So that it could be taken on a 12-day tour of the United States for people to pay their last respects to their murdered leader. Lincoln's mummy was last seen in 1871, when his preserved body was said to be in good condition.

◄ A company in Salt Lake City, Utah, offers people the chance to be mummified, wrapped in cotton, covered with fiberglass, and then placed inside a body-shaped metal coffin.

► The mummy of Lenin is displayed in Moscow, Russia. As the years have passed politics and ideas have changed, and one day Lenin's body may be buried.

Mummies of communist leaders

Vladimir Ilyich Lenin led the Russian Revolution. When he died in 1924, his body was embalmed in a secret process and then put on display. It was a way of saying that Lenin had not completely departed from this world—he was still among the living. It started a trend among communist leaders. Lenin's successor, Joseph Stalin, was embalmed and displayed in 1953. The preserved body of Ho Chi Minh, leader of North Vietnam, was displayed in 1969, and in 1976 300,000 people went to see the mummy of Mao Zedong, China's dead leader.

▲ Eva Perón, wife of the president of Argentina, died in 1952. Her body was embalmed. In 1955 the Argentine government was overthrown, and Eva's mummy went to Europe for safekeeping. It was returned to Argentina in 1974.

The train robber who became a mummy

Elmer J. McCurdy was shot dead in 1911 in Oklahoma after robbing a train. His body was embalmed with arsenic, but instead of being buried it toured the U.S. with a carnival. In 1976 a movie crew used the mummy in a TV show. They thought it was only a scary dummy, but when an arm fell off, the grisly truth was revealed. McCurdy was then buried, putting an end to the mummy's travels.

An Egyptian mummy made in the U.S.

We can learn about the past by recreating something that happened long ago—such as Egyptian-style mummification. In the 1990s American scientists mummified the body of a 76-year-old man using the techniques and replica tools of the ancient Egyptians (see pages 18–21). His organs were removed, and he was covered with natron. When dry, his body was wrapped in linen.

This unique experiment has revealed information that cannot be learned by studying old mummies. For example, it was found that a body loses more than half of its weight after it is dried out with natron.

Mummy mania

Mummies can grip public imagination. Movie studios have cast them as heroes and villains (the first mummy movie, made in France, came out in 1909), countless books have been written about them, and artists have been inspired by their unusual looks (*The Scream*, painted by Norwegian artist Edvard Munch, is based on a mummy's facial expression). And there are many stories about curses and strange occurrences.

"Death comes on wings to he who enters . . .

. . . the tomb of a pharaoh." Who says so? In 1923 an English novelist, Marie Corelli, wrote to *The Times* newspaper in London, claiming that this was an ancient curse (in fact, she had made it up). The tomb of pharaoh Tutankhamen had recently been found, and Corelli predicted death for anyone who entered it. When a mosquito bite led to the death of Lord Carnarvon, the excavation sponsor, it was taken as proof of the curse. Even today some people still believe in the idea of a "mummy's curse."

◄ It took eight hours for the makeup team to transform English actor Boris Karloff (real name William Henry Pratt) into a bandaged and wrinkled mummy for the movie *The Mummy* (1932).

▲ Movie poster for *The Mummy* (1932), in which Boris Karloff played two roles. In one role he was Im-Ho-Tep, an Egyptian mummy. In the other he was Ardath Bey—the mummy reborn as a person in the present day. At the time of its release the *New York Times* newspaper said it was: ". . . one of the most unusual talkies ever produced." It left audiences on the edge of their seats.

The mummy as an "urban myth"

It was a cursed mummy that caused the ship *Titanic* to collide with an iceberg and sink in 1912 on its first voyage. True or false? False, of course! However, some people have actually fallen for this urban myth (a story that sounds as if it could be true but is not).

These are the true facts behind the strange case of the so-called "Unlucky Mummy." The British Museum in London, England, has an ancient Egyptian coffin lid in its collection—but not the mummy of the woman it once covered. In the early 1900s William Stead, an English journalist, and Thomas Murray, an amateur Egyptologist, became interested in the lid, which was said to be unlucky (bad luck was supposed to happen to anyone linked with it).

Stead wrote about the coffin lid and its powers. Later Stead died on the *Titanic* (certainly bad luck). Survivors said he had entertained passengers with his "Unlucky Mummy" story. As often happens with stories, new parts were added as it was told again and again, and Stead's story took on a life of its own. It was said that the British Museum had wanted to get rid of a cursed mummy (this sounded more exciting than saying a "coffin lid"). They sold the make-believe mummy to an American, who shipped it across the Atlantic Ocean on—you guessed it—the *Titanic*.

The truth is that the lid never went anywhere. It is on display today in the British Museum, just as it has been since 1890.

► It was this decorated coffin lid (item number 22542) in the British Museum that became mixed up in the urban myth about the existence of a mummy onboard the ill-fated ocean liner *Titanic*. Despite attempts to tell the truth, the story still crops up, and people still fall for the joke. Or perhaps they are the type of people who just want to believe it is true, no matter what they are told.

▼ In the blockbuster movie *The Mummy Returns* (2001) a 3,000-year-old Egyptian mummy turns up "alive" in 1935 and immediately begins stirring up trouble.

Learning from mummies

Their hearts stopped beating long ago, their voices fell silent, and the worlds they knew vanished. But all is not lost. We have inherited their physical remains, and from their preserved bodies we can learn a lot about them— the lives they led and the worlds they knew. These mummies, who were once living beings, bring us something more precious than gold, more fleeting than life itself—they bring us information. In the same way that ancient people asked questions about their world we now ask questions about them—and their mummified bodies provide us with answers.

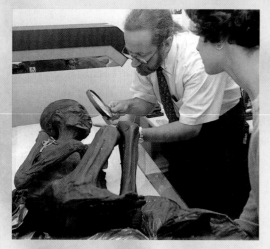

▲ A mummy from Peru is examined by scientists in the U.S. As part of the examination the 1,000-year-old mummy was given a bone scan, in which its skeleton was studied in detail, looking for signs of ancient disease and injury.

The study of ancient suffering

A rapidly developing area in the study of mummies is paleopathology. Meaning "ancient suffering," it is the study of diseases and injuries that people had in the past. The science of paleopathology is around 100 years old. In the early days X ray was the main form of scientific examination. X rays were, and still are, used to study mummies' bones. As new techniques have been developed it is now possible to study the soft tissue of mummies—the very "stuff" preserved by the mummification process.

Mummies are our teachers

Mummies teach us about diseases such as the lung disease tuberculosis. By comparing mummies with modern people it is possible to see whether or not today's illnesses are the result of present-day lifestyles. A person with a stressful life or a high-fat diet may get vein disease. It was once thought this was a modern problem—but the clogged-up veins of mummies show that the ancient Egyptians had it too.

▼ Dr. Margaret Murray (second from right) was one of the first archaeologists to study mummies scientifically. In this photograph, taken in 1908, she is seen at the unwrapping and examination of a mummy at Manchester Museum in England.

◀ Lying inside its decorated coffin is a wrapped Egyptian mummy. Using today's high-tech medical equipment, such as this computerized axial tomography (CAT) scanner, it is possible to take pictures of the body inside the wrappings without any need to open the coffin or unwrap the mummy.

Cloning mummies

An intriguing study of human mummies is in the area of genetics. Scientists have isolated the genetic material known as deoxyribonucleic acid (DNA) from the cells of Egyptian mummies. DNA is the "building block" of life, which, in humans, is a code made up of six billion different units. We inherit DNA from our parents, and we pass it on to our children. Locked inside our cells is DNA that existed when the first humans evolved, when the Egyptians built their pyramids, when Columbus reached the Americas, and so on. By recovering ancient human DNA and "growing" it in a laboratory it is possible to make an exact copy (clone) of part of a person's genetic code. This provides information that can be used to figure out family ties. Being able to say who was related to whom among Egyptian pharaohs and families will answer puzzles that cannot be solved in any other way.

We are what we eat

Diet plays a major role in our well-being. A bad diet leaves signs on our bodies— too much fat leads to obesity; too much sugar causes tooth decay; too much salt can damage our hearts. But diet-related problems are not unique to us. The worn teeth found in the skulls of ancient Egyptians and the bog bodies of northern Europe, such as Grauballe Man from Denmark, are clear signs that ancient diets included abrasive substances that were rough enough to wear away tooth enamel, making cavities that would have led to toothaches and painful abscesses. And what was the cause of this? Most likely it was grit and sand mixed up in people's food, especially bread.

◀ Is this the face of Tutankhamen? In 2002 the boy king's face was reconstructed, based on measurements taken of his skull (his mummy was unwrapped in 1925). A digital image was first created, from which an artist built this clay head.

The life and death of Mummy 1770

Once she had a name. Her parents had given it to her, and she answered them when they called her by it. Her name was an essential part of who she was. It was more than simply a label. Her parents put effort into choosing it. Perhaps they chose a name they hoped would bring their daughter good fortune in life; or a name that would protect her from harm; or a name that gave thanks to the gods for her life. But that name is now lost, and the teenage girl whose life was cut short is today simply labeled as "Mummy 1770."

▲ These false legs, made from bundles of reeds and mud wrapped in linen, were attached to the stumps of Mummy 1770's legs.

◀ She cannot have known that the water she sipped from the Nile river contained the larvae of the guinea worm, a parasite that lives inside the body until it emerges as an adult through the lower legs. Were her legs amputated because of the pain this worm caused her?

The examination of Mummy 1770

Mummy 1770 lived and died in Egypt. Before her body was examined in 1975 by Dr. Rosalie David and her team at Manchester Museum in England, it was thought that she had died around A.D. 200, when the craft of mummy making was going out of fashion in Egypt. However, the examination changed this idea. When her bones were dated by radiocarbon analysis, it showed she had died around 1000 B.C.

▲ The girl's fingers were covered in finger stalls. Made from thin sheets of pure gold, this form of body adornment was expensive—a sign that she was from a wealthy family.

The rewrapped mummy

As her wrappings were removed it became clear that there was no soft tissue preserved on the bones—the "mummy" was not much more than a skeleton. Paint on her skull indicated that her body—what was left of it—had already been reduced to bones by the time it was wrapped. But there was a puzzle—the radiocarbon date for her bones (c.1000 B.C.) did not match the date of the linen wrappings (c. A.D. 380). Her body was already 1,400 years old when it was wrapped! It seems that she must have been rewrapped in new linen centuries after her death, perhaps because she was someone of importance.

Mystery of the missing legs

It was known from X rays taken before the unwrapping that the girl's legs were missing from the knees. As the linen wrappings came off Dr. David and her team discovered that the girl had been given false legs made out of reeds and mud. Her body had been "rebuilt" so that she could be whole again in her new life after death. The question then was—how had she lost her legs?

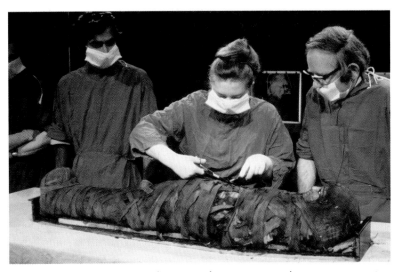

▲ Dr. Rosalie David begins to remove the wrappings from Mummy 1770. The team wore surgeons' gowns, masks, and gloves—they did not want to risk contaminating the mummy with anything from the present day, and they did not want to inhale any dust from the 3,000-year-old remains.

Once upon a time . . .

Scientific evidence helps us understand the past, but sometimes it raises more questions than it answers. The case of Mummy 1770's missing legs is an example of this. Several theories exist to explain how she lost them. One is that she drowned in the Nile river, and her legs were chewed off by a crocodile or a hippopotamus. The problem with this theory is that a crocodile does not bite through bone; it twists a limb until it tears off at a joint (a leg would break off at the hip). Another idea is that she was injured in an accident—perhaps her legs were crushed when something heavy fell on them such as a block of stone. Or perhaps they were cut off by doctors because they were covered in painful sores from guinea worms—parasites that had infected the girl's body and which were found in her mummy. What do you think?

Misused mummies

We have come a long way since mummies were treated as objects of curiosity, unwrapped, unraveled, and unrolled as public entertainment for paying audiences. No longer are their withered remains ground up and used as medicine, daubed across artists' canvases as a unique shade of brown paint, or scattered over farmers' fields as fertilizer. Now we care for mummies and treat them with respect. We also learn from them. But even today there are those who plunder their resting places—just like the tomb robbers of the past.

◀ Until the early 1900s Egyptian mummies were crushed into a fine brown powder that was mixed with oil to become an artists' paint known as "Mummy Brown." It was used in Europe for hundreds of years—until the paint makers ran out of mummies. The famous Victorian artist Edward Burne-Jones was so horrified when he discovered what was inside of his paint tube that he gave it a proper burial in his garden—with a daisy on its grave!

▼ This is a mummy of the Guanche culture from the Canary Islands, off the coast of West Africa. The Guanche people were the original inhabitants of the islands. They mummified the bodies of leaders and nobles in a style similar to that of the ancient Egyptians. After removing the internal organs and brain the body was dried in the sun or over a fire. Then the empty body cavity was filled with plants and other stuffing materials, the embalmers' cut was sewn up, and the body was wrapped in skins and placed in a burial cave. The Guanche made mummies for 1,000 years until the 1400s.

Mummies as medicine

Out of the thousands of mummies that once rested in peace in caves on the Canary Islands, no more than around 20 now exist. These are the bodies of the Guanche people—one of the world's last mummy-making cultures. The rest were destroyed by Spanish conquerors in the 1400s. Others were sent to Europe where, in the 1500s, they were made into powder and used in medicines—yuck! The same fate awaited many Egyptian mummies. Mummy medicine was thought to cure many illnesses. It tasted terrible, but the sick, desperate to be cured, still took it.

Raiders of the lost artifacts

If you thought tomb raiders only existed in the past—or only in computer games and movies—it is time to think again. Somewhere in the world today they are hard at work, plundering tombs that archaeologists do not know about. However, all is not lost. Sometimes, when the looted objects are offered for sale, archaeologists can trace them back to where they came from—and this may lead them to a mummy. This is how the mummies of many Egyptian pharaohs were found in 1881 and 1898 (see page 25). Like vultures hovering over their prey, the activity of looters often attracts the attention of experts.

Feline fertilizer—recycling old mummies

In the 1800s Great Britain's population grew from 10 million to 37 million. With extra mouths to feed, farmers were forced to plow more land than ever before. In order to increase the yield of their crops they added fertilizer to the soil to improve it. And what was that fertilizer made from? Shockingly, the ground-up bodies of animal mummies from ancient Egypt—especially cats and birds! One 17-ton shipment contained the crushed corpses of 180,000 mummified cats. The Victorians would not have been amused if they had known what had been fed to the food that they had then eaten!

▲ Looting of ancient burial grounds is a worldwide problem. Tomb raiders do not care about the human remains they disturb, instead they steal objects from graves that they can sell on the illegal antiquities market. When a grave, such as the one in Peru shown above, has been disturbed in this way, valuable information is lost forever.

◄ This is a carefully wrapped mummy of an ibis, a bird that was sacred to the ancient Egyptians. Millions of ibis mummies were buried at Saqqâra, near Cairo in Egypt. In the 1800s many were destroyed when their bodies were recycled to use as fertilizers for farmers' fields.

What's black and white and dead all over?

Have you heard the story about the Egyptian mummy wrappings that were sent to the U.S. where they were made into paper? This is what is said to have happened in the 1850s, when mummies were shipped to American paper mills (at this time paper was made from rags, not wood pulp). The mummies were unwrapped, and their linen wrappings were supposedly made into paper—the *Syracuse Standard* newspaper is said to have printed an entire issue on it! Really? You must be joking! None of this has ever been proved—it is just another mummy myth.

Craft of the mummy fakers

In the murky world of mummy merchants—traders who have sold mummies for medicine, paint, and fertilizer—bad things have happened. When there were not enough old mummies to sell to Europe's apothecaries (medicine makers), merchants in Alexandria, Egypt, found a way around the shortage. They took corpses that no one wanted—executed criminals, the poor, the diseased. And when these body snatchers had their prey, they embalmed and wrapped them and pretended they were mummies of ancient Egyptians. In 1564 a French doctor, Guy de la Fontaine, who had ordered a lot of mummies, became suspicious because they smelled rotten, like meat that had recently spoiled. The trader admitted that they were fakes—not one was more than four years dead.

A "Persian princess" from Pakistan

Mummy faking still happens. In October 2000 police in Pakistan raided a house near the Afghan and Iranian borders. Inside they found the mummy of a woman. It was for sale on the illegal antiquities market. An inscription on her coffin said that she was Princess Rhodugune, daughter of Xerxes I, king of Persia. Wrapped in linen strips in the style of the mummies of ancient Egypt, she wore a gold crown and mask. It was an incredible discovery. There, it seemed, was the first mummy from Pakistan—the 2,500-year-old daughter of a great king. The Pakistani authorities declared the mummy a national treasure and took it to the Archaeology Museum in Karachi for examination. They were stunned by what they found . . .

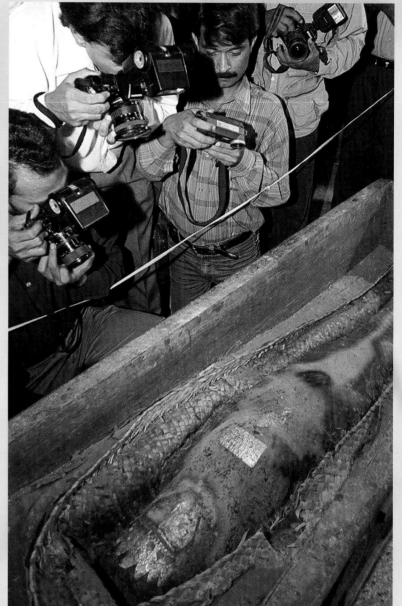

▲ The "Princess Rhodugune" mummy. Its discovery made news headlines around the world—but all was not as it seemed. Inside the wrappings lay the modern body of a young woman who had been murdered. Criminals planned to sell her mummy for millions of dollars.

▲ No longer destined to be made into fertilizer, this cat mummy from ancient Egypt fascinates visitors to the museum where it is now on display. There it will be safe for the future, cared for by the museum's curators and conservators, far out of reach of tomb robbers.

The truth behind the mummy of "Princess Rhodugune"

Suspicions were soon raised about the "Persian princess." It was thought that she had been mummified by Egyptian embalmers. Her organs and brain had been removed—but so had her heart, which the Egyptians were careful to leave in the body (see page 19). In addition, the coffin inscription had mistakes in it. A CAT scan (see page 53) revealed the awful truth—inside the mummy's wrappings was a modern body. A woman had been killed and mummified. The Pakistani police have not yet solved this terrible crime.

SUMMARY OF CHAPTER 4: MUMMIES TODAY

Are mummies still made today?

We live in a world where mummies are still being made. The bodies of some of the world's leaders have been artificially preserved by embalmers, and their mummies have been put on display for the public to view. Even ordinary people are being turned into mummies. One man donated his body to science so that it could be mummified in the same way as that of an ancient Egyptian—this is an example of experimental archaeology. In another case a woman was murdered and her body was turned into a mummy that was supposed to trick people into thinking she was a 2,500-year-old princess—this is an example of mummy faking.

How have mummies been treated?

Mummies of humans and animals have not always been treated with respect by later generations, who have used them as raw materials in medicine, paint, and agricultural fertilizer. They have been cast in the role of agents of harm, cursing all who dare to interfere with them, as well as taking center stage in movies and other works of fiction.

What can we learn from mummies?

Scientists are able to, literally, get beneath the skin of a mummy. X-ray machines show a mummy's skeleton, revealing injuries to bones that give us clues about the person's lifestyle and, maybe, the that work he or she did. CAT scans show us the parts that X rays cannot reach, revealing internal organs and other soft tissue, from which we can learn about ancient diseases and compare them with ones in modern people. Mummies are time capsules through which we are able to see not only the faces of the past but also the past itself. And by understanding the past we are able to make more sense of the present— the world in which we live—and which we will hand down to our children and to our children's children.

Go further . . .

For the Animal Mummy Project in Cairo, Egypt, go to:
www.animalmummies.com

Read more about mummification today at: www.summum.org/mummification/

For the full story about the fake mummy "Princess Rhodugune" go to:
www.bbc.co.uk/science/horizon/2001/persianmummy.shtml

For older readers:
Conversations with Mummies by Dr. Rosalie David & Rick Archbold (The Madison Press Ltd, 2000)

Forensic scientist
Skilled in DNA fingerprinting— examining cells in a mummy to find out more about its past.

Radiologist
Carries out X rays and CAT scans, that can take pictures of inside a mummy or mummy case so that scientists can examine it in detail.

Reconstruction artist
Skilled in reconstructing a face from an X ray, CAT scan, or mummified head so that we can see what the mummy looked like when he or she was alive.

Lenin can be seen at the Lenin Mausoleum.
www.leninmausoleum.da.ru
Lenin Mausoleum
Red Square, Moscow

The "Unlucky Mummy" can be seen in the British Museum in London, England.
www.thebritishmuseum.ac.uk
British Museum
London, England WC1B 3DG
Phone: 44 20 7323 8299

The American Dime Museum displays fake and real mummies.
www.dimemuseum.com
Baltimore, MD 21201
Phone: (410) 230-0263

Glossary

abdomen
The lower half of the main part of your body that contains your kidneys and digestive organs.

afterlife
The idea that after a person dies a part of them continues to exist in a new life after death.

amulet
Object worn as a protective device or "lucky charm" to ward off evil.

ancestors
Relatives who lived hundreds or thousands of years ago.

archaeologist
Someone who studies the remains of the past.

arthritis
A condition that causes pain and swelling of the joints.

artificial
Something that is man-made.

autopsies
Examinations of bodies after death to find out the cause of death.

bacteria
Tiny living things that are often the cause of diseases.

cartonnage
Linen stiffened with plaster, used to make mummy masks and coffins in ancient Egypt.

CAT scans
Pictures that are created using an electronic system called computerized axial tomography (CAT) that show the inside of a living or dead body without cutting it open.

cavity
A hollow place.

corpse
The dead body of a person or animal.

cremation
To burn a dead body to ashes.

crypt
A cellar under the floor of a church, often used as a burial place.

curse
To wish or cause evil or harm to someone or something.

decay
To rot.

decomposition
When something is rotting.

dehydrate
To remove moisture from something.

embalmers
People who preserve dead bodies of people or animals so that they will not rot.

environment
The surroundings and conditions of a place.

excavated
To be uncovered by digging up.

exhumed
To have dug up a body from its place of burial.

fiberglass
A strong, man-made material made from melted glass.

flints
Hard minerals shaped and used by ancient peoples to light fires or as tools or weapons.

genetics
The science of inherited family characteristics.

gilded
Covered with gold or a goldlike substance.

glacier
A large, slow-moving mass of ice.

inherited
When an object is handed down from relative to relative at death or when a characteristic, such as eye color, is passed on to children by their parents.

inscription
Something cut or engraved into a substance such as stone or wood.

intestines
The body's digestive system.

kidneys
Vital organs in a person's abdomen.

liver
The largest vital organ in the body.

maggots
Larvae of certain insects, especially flies, that feed on decaying flesh.

mineral
A natural substance in Earth's surface.

miracle
A dramatic and surprising event that cannot be explained.

natron
A natural, saltlike substance found in old lake beds in ancient Egypt. It was a main part of the Egyptian mummification process because it dried out a body when placed on it for a long period of time.

organic
A naturally occurring substance.

organs
Important parts of the body, such as the heart, that carry out different roles.

pagan
A person who does not believe in God.

peat
A soillike substance made from decayed vegetable matter found in bogs. Commonly cut into blocks, dried, and used as fuel.

perforated
Having many small holes.

pharaoh
A ruler or god king of ancient Egypt.

preserved
To be kept or guarded against decay either naturally or deliberately.

pyre
A pile of flammable material, such as wood, on which a dead body is cremated.

radiocarbon
A substance called carbon 14. Radiocarbon dating is used by scientists to find out the age of any organic material, such as body tissue, by measuring the amount of carbon 14 still remaining.

reign
The time when a monarch, such as a pharaoh, once ruled.

replica
An exact copy of something.

resin
A very sticky substance that oozes from pine trees.

sacred
Something that is holy or very respected that should not be harmed in any way.

sacrifice
When a person or animal is killed as an offering to a god.

sarcophagus
The outermost section of a coffin, which is made out of stone for better protection. From a Greek word meaning "flesh eater."

subterranean
Underground.

swabs
Small, bundled pieces of material used to put oils and resins onto bodies.

tattoos
A colored design on skin made by pricking holes on the skin's surface and filling them with color such as ink.

theories
Explanations that have been put forward but have not been proved true.

tinder
Dry substances that catch fire from a spark.

tissue
The substance of a plant or body, such as fat or muscle, of which parts of bodies are made.

tomb
A grave.

torso
The upper half of the body above the hips but not the head or arms.

wedjat eye
In ancient Egypt the left eye of Horus. It symbolized the power of healing and was a powerful amulet.

X ray
A photograph of the bones inside a body.

Index

Acknowledgments

The publisher would like to thank the following for permission to reproduce their material. Every care has been taken to trace copyright holders. However, if there have been unintentional omissions or failure to trace copyright holders, we apologize and will, if informed, endeavor to make corrections in any future edition.

Key: *b* = bottom, *c* = center, *l* = left, *r* = right, *t* = top

pages: *front cover* (left to right) Werner Forman Archive/The Greenland Museum, Art Archive, Corbis; *back cover* British Museum; *title page* Corbis; 2–3 Corbis; 4–5 National Geographic Image Collection (NGIC); 7 Corbis; 8*tl* The Bridgeman Art Library/Louvre, Paris, France; 8*bl* Corbis; 9*tl* Associated Press (AP); 9*br* Corbis; 10–11 Dr. Joann Fletcher; 12*tl* South Tyrol Museum of Archaeology, Bolzano, Italy; 13*br* Corbis/Sygma; 14*cl* Corbis; 15 Art Archive; 16–17 British Museum; 16*tr* Corbis; 17*tr* Corbis; 18*bl* Corbis; 19*tr* British Museum; 19*c* Topham/Heritage Image Partnership; 19*b* Science Photo Library (SPL); 20*cl* British Museum; 20*bl* Art Archive; 20*br* British Museum; 21*t* SPL; 21*br* British Museum; 22*tl* AKG, London; 22*tr* British Museum; 23 Hulton Getty; 24*tl* Musée du Caire Catalogue/The Oriental Institute, The University of Chicago; 24*tr* Musée du Caire Catalogue/The Oriental Institute, The University of Chicago; 24–25 NGIC; 25*tr* Corbis; 26*tl* The Manchester Museum, University of Manchester; 26*bl* Musée du Caire Catalogue/The Oriental Institute, The University of Chicago; 27*l* Musée du Caire Catalogue/The Oriental Institute, The University of Chicago; 27*tr* Art Archive; 27*br* AP; 28*l* Corbis; 28*b* Corbis; 28–29 British Museum; 29 British Museum; 30*cl* British Museum; 31 SPL; 32*tl* SPL; 32*b* Corbis; 33*tr* British Museum; 33*br* SPL; 34–35 NGIC; 34*tl* Art Archive; 35*tr* Kimberley King; 35*br* Art Archive; 36*bl* Werner Forman Archive/The Greenland Museum; 36*tr* AP; 37*tr* Corbis; 37*bl* Dr. Owen Beattie; 38*tl* Corbis; 38*bl* Corbis; 39*tr* Rex Features; 40*tl* Corbis/Sygma; 40*cl* Hulton Getty; 40–41 Corbis/Sygma; 41*tr* Press Association; 41*cl* Press Association; 42 Corbis; 43 Corbis; 44*bl* Charles Sternberg, Wyoming; 44–45 Corbis; 45*tr* Corbis; 45*br* Salisbury and South Wiltshire Museum; 46*cl* AP; 47 Hulton Getty; 48*l* Summum Institute, U.S.; 48–49 AP; 49*t* Rex Features; 50*l* AP; 50*br* Corbis; 51*bl* Kobal; 51*r* British Museum; 52*tl* AP; 52*bl* The Manchester Museum, University of Manchester; 53*t* SPL; 53*b* Science & Society Picture Library; 54*bl* The Manchester Museum, University of Manchester; 54*tr* The Manchester Museum, University of Manchester; 55*tr* The Manchester Museum, University of Manchester; 56*tr* Fitzwilliam Museum; 56*b* Corbis; 57*t* SPL; 57*b* The Bridgeman Art Library/Ashmolean Museum, Oxford; 58*tr* Press Association; 58*bl* AP; 59*cr* Rex Features; 60 Musée du Caire Catalogue/The Oriental Institute, The University of Chicago; 61 AP; 64 Werner Forman Archive/The Greenland Museum.

The publisher would like to thank the following illustrators:
Bruce Emmett/Folio 12–13, 38–39, 54–55

The author and publisher would like to thank Dr. Joann Fletcher for her expert assistance.

The author wishes to thank Carron Brown for her skillful editing and encouragement.

"Every time I eat a raisin, I think of it as the mummy of a grape."
– John Malam

To contact the author write to: johnmalam@aol.com